PRECIOUS CARGO

ADAM LOWE
&
SUE SHAW

Published by
Fruit Bruise Press
an imprint of
Dog Horn Publishing
45 Monk Ings
Birstall
Batley
WF17 9HU
doghornpublishing.com

Typesetting by
Adam Lowe

Cover design by
Adam Lowe

Covert art:
Detail from *Woodpecker* tapestry designed by William Morris.

Distribution: Central Books
99 Wallis Road, London, E9 5LN, United Kingdom
orders@centralbooks.com
Phone:+44 (0) 845 458 9911
Fax: +44 (0) 845 458 9912

SECTION ONE

ADAM LOWE

JOSEPH DALTON HOOKER

Can you see it yet? Spread in the fists
of violet and scarlet. Can you see it yet?
Written in an ink of dew, nectar, honey
—the inevitable reach of frailty to perfection.

Can you see it yet, laid out before you?
Rising bold as stars from the ground
in layers of pink and yellow? Can you see it
writ in the language of the *Genera Plantarum*?

Can you see it the way nature meant it?
From chaos, order. From innocence, experience.
Turned out, an ongoing process, yearning for divinity.
Can you see it yet, this glory before us?

AT THE ROSE-TREE

I remove my sandals, kneel at the feet
of this tree of roses, its constellate boughs burning
with sweet pink flames, circular crowns.

Its occult alchemy speaks of the exultation
of nature, declares a fierce botany of the sublime,
sheds petals, letters shaped like ritual knives,

the sacred name: *rhodon, dendron*. Tree of roses
that cuts to the quick, releases blood
spatter of pink stars on the galaxy's spiral arm.

Cartwheeling rhododendron intoxicates, promises a mouthful
of Turkish delight in rolling syllables, the mythic opium kiss
of enchanted slumber, unfolding fire in the night.

LUCIFER:

firelight; a blood diamond raised
high, poised with pride; draws terrible
wings, flights of red, clipped, becomes
a falling bough heavy with the burden
of morning dew, a shooting star, arcing,
hits—compacted to a brooch in the ground.

RHODODENDRON BARBATUM

Vibrant crimson, water-
melon sorbet, flutters
in spring breezes like a flamenco
dancer's skirt, seeded with
promise—a story ready
to embark on its journey
and settle, take root, in
the heart of some place new.

SPRING

Blossoms dance from the branch
in a flutter of silk snow. The tree
catches, a spiny note, in spring's breath.

FROM THE TREE

(after Moniza Alvi's 'A Bowl of Warm Air')

Somersault from bough, gravid with knowing
pulp and the pip-weight of rot. Roll far
from the root, weighty with revolution's insistence,
too fast for maggots or piglets to trough.

Those who reach grasp only bowls of warm air,
must content self with orchard bruises,
and must watch as you spin a crooked arc
at odds to the brushstroke symmetry of branches

and trunk. You flash, a blood-red moon,
or the sluagh in gloom; unreadable
as you capture the still world behind you
and the frozen world in front.

IN THE STUMPERY

Lucy took her lover, fled
to the sanctuary of forest,
and tangled as lovers do on the
ground. But the fairy curse
of what they had become among
toadstools, turned them hard
as oak. In no time they
were the roots of trees, knotted
branches, nevertheless yearning
to become the antlered crowns
of regal stags—fingernails,
lightning jags—fibrous, smooth,
then rough, cracked geometries, cast
in yellow-browns, green-greys,
fungal white, blood reds, purple hues—
become a nest for monstrous birds,
perhaps a pterodactyl, where
the terror of liberty for a young girl
grows gnarled, a stumpery, cut short—

GARDEN

Beneath a quilt of snow, I lie
still, shiver, at rest. The crisp
taste of dripping water from
the frozen fingers of sycamore
awakens me, washes the pale
sleep from my eyes.
              My eyes are blue,
bells that ring, delicate,
shake the bones of the trees.

It is him again, come to
woo, his golden eye a tiger's,
fierce, treasure showered
over me.
        He licks away the thick
of slumber, peels back the layers,
to allow my pores to open: crocuses
at first; then iris, daffodils, celandine.
Their networks of roots yearning
for the deep of me, hungry.

In his radiance, I blush:
drape myself in a robe of roses,
adorn with a brooch of rhododendron,
crown with muscat vines.
                  He fills me
with glory, which nourishes
a sea of pink and yellow, silver and scarlet.
Open blooms ripple like goosebumps
over my skin. He sends
armies of butterflies to serenade
the trembling colour of me.
                    In his light
I thrive, ebulliently alive, and dream
of slow clouds slipping over me.

THE MARRIAGE VOW

In the shade we fold into the dark bows of limbs,
our shadows pool among roots. Succumbing, you pull
from the low-slung branch plump bulbs of light.
Your knife orbits the golden fruit, disrobes

its pithy sunlight. You give it to me:
a half-moon, a swell bowl of jewels,
a fistful of princely favour. This dowry made
in bright strands of citrus fibre.

Illuminated, the canopy of the blossoming tree
becomes sanctuary no more, exposes dark ridges
of flesh, wet, scattered with seeds, anointed
with juice that beads and runs where it will.

I am hungry. You feed me discus after discus,
mandarin quavers. There is no time to discuss
the flavour. Just fill the hollow at my collarbone,
a liquid necklace; make me your shining queen.

LIGHTNING TREE

Once you were verdant,
proudly bristling with emerald
pendants, until lightning struck.

Flayed of bark
and leaves, left a gnarled,
scoliotic skeleton, protean

and bald, as though racked
by cancer. But lightning
never strikes twice, so

maybe now it's time
to grow. See the moss
flourishes, a new skin

across your splintered bones
and the kingfisher loves you,
for your support

and your inelegant beauty.
So let me tend you.
Let me love you again.

AMBERGRIS

You were ambergris:
slipping white marble

train, shuffling chiffon
from the rear of a whale;

tossed among waves
and tentacling like

viscous mist down
to sandy bottoms where

petrified of pearly eyes
you turned to stone.

Soon you were washed up,
cast upon shore, hunchbacked

Picasso nude. Concrete poetry.
But I found you, strewn

among shingle, misshapen
Rosetta, revealing the code

of want. I wrapped you
in my coat, precious cargo,

salvage I couldn't fathom.
I warmed you beneath

my tongue, you became
tender again, took on glorious

sunshine aureole, pot of
gold in the shallows; I bent

rainbow over you.
I longed to be over

you as you begged
to be consumed.

You got inside me, turned
poison, waxy, paraffin;

made me spew in tidal
waves polluted surf; adrift;

flotsam feeling jetsam;
shipwrecked to the core.

FACES

I deserted, fled my station in
the drawing room, holding my skirts

above my ankles like a savage,
like Boudicca. It was to feel the whip

of cold, fresh air, to know the taste
of autumn, to smell the musk

of deer. It was to be one with the
wild things. I watched for new faces

between the trees: owlish ovals with
gold-green eyes, squirrels furiously

devouring nuts, a stag regarding the lay
of the land like a king under branches.

Everyday, inside the house, I saw those
same cloistered masques, poker faces,

obeisant keepers, my husband's nose
cocked like his rifle. But it wasn't enough.

So I stole a chisel from the servants'
quarters and ran to the deer shed where

I reclined, and there dug, an archaeologist,
into the very stone, to find new faces

that might smile at me, that might
provide original company. And as I saw

their cherubic faces emerge, I knew
which faces I wanted. I clutched

at my midriff, watched by the pheasants,
and for the first time discovered I was crowded.

FLOWERS

We choose to eat flowers together,
starting with damask roses.

You swallow the dandelions
with a grimace at the tang,

and bite the heads off lilies
like Barbie losing her skirts.

But our favourites are the silverbells
that ring in our ears for days.

ROOTS

Roots run deep, wherever I see them, they remind me
of this sticky horse chestnut tree grown mad and wild
here in my father's garden. Its roots burrow through soil,
beneath a haphazard stumpery puzzled together from
crooked hair clippings. The knotted mess a confused cat's cradle
of memories, grazed knees, climbing trees, stone-throwing,
war over scarce resources (conkers, usually, in bristling spiked helmets).
Now the tangle cuts deeper than the grazes if I try to navigate
its pathways back. Beyond the trees, a sea of rusted Hondas,
Yamahas, Suzukis, a steel-plated door. The house facia is cracked,
threatens to split my childhood in two. The house I grew up in.
And inside, he gathers, gathers, gathers. He presides and festers.
His own empire that won't speak of the things I have felt and have seen.

SABLE

He returns, a black knight in Mongol fur,
his face the colour of sap. He smells like felled trees,
encrusted at the rim by ocean salt,
hands fixed like bear claws. He is sable,

alien before the hearth, with a tang of accent
I can't understand, and his veins grown thick
as roots across his burnished saffron skin.
What have I let in? This savage wearing

the flesh of my husband, who stinks
of standing water, rancid meat, the sweat
of a thousand mile journey? His lips spread thin,
a garden provoked to bloom, spring to summer,

and I see him, the bristling stamen in irises,
familiar—and he wears cotton shirts again.
Those far lands have changed the edges,
but the centre, although travelled, is the same.

TO MAKE A FORTUNE

Robert of Scotland left Chiswick,
turning from the Horticultural Society's
tea parties and pollen, to venture to jasmine
trails. There, as tigers and dragons slept,

he fled from pirate fleets, quick
as sails could muster, but still
pursued, caught, at last shipwrecked,
turned back to shore. But he had

a plan. A clever disguise to avoid
capture, water torture, for the sake
of a few petals, the unguent of
nectar. So he returned, crowned

curator of Chelsea Physic Gardens,
then recruited finally by the East India
Company to investigate tea, transplant
then stitch it in new lands of saffron.

His life became more private, but
locked up in history books, remembered
by pirates, he spent the rest of his life
behind glass, a bulb in a Wardian case.

BAT'S FLIGHT THROUGH
WENTWORTH CASTLE GARDENS, MIDNIGHT

You unfold leather wings along
skyline, smouldering black rose,
cut night with your thorns, serrated
blossom chasing catcalls silent
to normal ears. The buds of hearing
spread to oily inverse sunlight, cherish
the throng of slumber and plight. Kite
frame of cartilaginous grace, spread
out like dark leaves, you fan the cloister
of air and feast on secrets, insects, grave.

BATH CHAIR

Sarcophagous of iron gapes
grim, a chariot of death,
rattling through the gardens,
hooded, steered by the grin
of rictus, the old madame,
cutting like a scythe across
the lawn. She thunders;
eyes glimmer darkly, resist
the lull of dust. Bound,
she is a menace, spectral,
chasing cats, manservant pushing
at her back as she thirsts
for blood to rejuvenate old bones.

SNOW

She drifts in like Asiatic navona and avalanche
roses, a train of cotton, the whispery hem
of a ghost's flapping sheet; slant

and slow, busted feathers, falling
from melancholic angels painted
in regency pale. They dissolve,

secrets. Shining bright as sunlight
even in its absence. Coddling fingers
of mistletoe, stark black

brushstrokes against her flesh. She is
a pillow, soft, comforting cold,
poised for shivering suffocation.

Her crystals dazzle and blind, unique
in their casual, spreading formations,
turned to tears come morning, on the bough.

SAPLINGS

I have a plant pot set aside
for you in the garden between
clematis and lilies. I pulled out
the weeds that had crept in there

and changed the soil, wet
and black between my fingers
like a gift from the River Styx
or Ecuadorian chocolate.

I take the photograph,
the only one I have of you,
and curl it into a celluloid tuber
which I bury like a secret.

I leave you there to germinate,
so those scant memories we have
can push through six feet of earth,
and flower as polaroids come spring.

SECTION TWO

SUE SHAW

THE £100 PINEAPPLE

The pineapple takes centre stage,
towers over tiers of peaches, figs and pears.
It requires only your admiration and servitude.
Smaller sized fruits are plucked from the display
and split open with delicately-designed dessert knives.

The pineapple shrugs smugly.
What knife can pierce its polished pinnacles?
What fork can spear such reptilian skin?
Scissors snip at vulnerable grape stems,
gaping mouths swallow and gulp.

The pineapple survives the dinner table,
borne away by a maid among lesser pips and peelings.
The housekeeper runs her fingertips
over the strangely sculptured surface;
pausing as superior soft-shoes approach.

The pineapple's silver salver
disappears in the butler's guiding hands,
prized possession of his padlocked pantry.
His expression places him above suspicion;
but sharp, sweet aromas tease his surly nostrils.

The pineapple waits prudishly on a small wooden table,
while the butler peels off both white gloves.
A spittle of saliva trickles from his lip
as he slides the strongest, sharpest blade from the block;
finally, he swallows hard and begins to carve.

AZALEA

Suspended, frothy
frill of spun silk, lemon pale,
cream-flecked party frock.

Faded fabric stains,
drooping, perfumed petals drop
tissued memories.

Bare-branched beeches watch
azalea budding blooms
long after the ball.

TARTE

First, pick your pear:
Doyenne du Comice or Beurre d'Anjou.
Flip its unbroken peel over your shoulder
to reveal a lover's initials
looped and coiled on lino.

Next, slice sharply and spiral
into a pastry case baked blind
(though without the aid of blackbirds),
to resemble overlapping, glossy feathers.
Shower in sugar with droppings of butter
and slip into the yawning heart of the oven.
Bake until so golden and fragrant,
your saliva rises like sweet sap
and tastebuds stand to attention.

Allow to cool by ignoring
(though this will be almost impossible),
until warm and moistly irresistible.
Cut a generously equilateral triangle
and cast adrift in a pool of cream.
Pause before wielding a spoon
and deny strenuously that you will consume
another slice before bedtime.

In your over-sweetened dreams,
the Doyenne du Comice sits by a guillotine;
gathering quartered pears in a basket.
You vow to avoid rich food late in the day.
In fact, best polish it off before lunchtime.

IVY

Gothic, waxen leaves
drop decorative drapes
to shroud the walled garden;
concealing feather-lined nests
and colonising cold frame corners.
Ivy smothers close-clipped hedges
and thrusts black beads against stained sky.

The gardener oils his secateurs,
approaching on spring-heeled steps.
Blades cut back clean and hard and deep,
halting the invasion of heartfelt leaves.
Winter's glossy evergreen burns reluctantly,
spitting and writhing in protest;
encircling him with slow blue smoke.

ONBOARD

He had no stomach for the sea, as it rose-and-fell, rose-and-fell in a swell around the ship. His body was a bottle shouldering the waves and his brain could receive no messages.

Stepping out onto dry land at last, the shore met him half way; heaving like a wave. Alone among the scientists, he stumbled on; tripping over an exquisite tangle of roots and boughs. Dazzling birds flitted in shots of neon, their faces cocked towards his in mutual wonder.

The ship was kinder on her return, allowing him sealegs to ride out the rhythm of unbroken waves. The rise-and-fall, rise-and-fall rocked him to sleep under Prussian blue billows riddled with stars.

Becalmed, he mapped out the abducted specimens stowed onboard. Sailors cursed when the ship clapped in irons, drifting listlessly through windless days. But his brush filled leaves and petals, roots and tendrils. He painted as though his life depended upon it, painted himself into the life he didn't know he had been longing for. Quickly, quickly, he raced against the wilting and fading.

The sails gently filled and the ship rose-and-fell, rose-and-fell with the swell once again. By day he circled the deck, spittled in sea spray; at night he dreamt of the impossibility of living on land ever again. Living without microscopic focus, or the strangely closed in and opened out parameters of a ship upon the sea.

He resolved to stay onboard, to stow away until the ship was too far from the harbour for a captain's return. He fell into a sleep without dreams; hammock-cocooned in the blissful moments before the storm.

CYCLAMEN

Snow drops from petals.
Bright unfurling faces nod
below startled trees.

CHERRY

Japanese tea cup,
Van Gogh's magenta emblem;
wind-blown confetti.

LILY

Trumpeting silence,
midnight's sacred lantern glow;
star-gazing seraph.

CROCOSMIA

Bright, bejewelled flame,
viridian spear plucked from
Lucifer's garden.

NOMENCLATURE

You inked their names fluently
in a leather-bound book:
Actimidia, Baptisia, Celastrus,
Dianthus, Eucomis, Fagopyrum,
Galtonia, Heuchera, Indocalamus.

You practised pronouncing each one,
as you strode the summer borders:
Justicia, Knautia, Lilium,
Mandragora, Nasella, Ophiopogon,
Phlomis, Roscoea, Senecio.

You thought of them carefully,
as characters in a Greek play.
Trachelospermum, Ulex, Valeriana,
Weigela, Yucca, Zantedeschia.

You resented the missing letters,
creating a midnight-blue bloom
in their absence:
Quenilium Xanthia.
Pictured by the Yangtze River,
her petals unfurl for gauzy moths
and fill the air with honeyed musk.
Rooted in your imagination,
you remember her more clearly
than any plant in your father's garden.

THE GLASS HOUSE

They inherited an overblown Muscat.
But she preferred potting compost and seed trays,
obedient lettuce in rows and tomatoes staked frequently.
He pruned and persuaded the vine, until it dripped grapes;
filling his new demijohns with sweetness
as she hoed, raked, dug and de-slugged
on the other side of the glass.

He chose three orchids and a kiwi,
clipped the vine lightly and designed a wine label.
She unearthed potatoes and harvested
other vegetables of good and reliable character.
He tapped the glass, beckoning her into his realm,
but she was unloading another barrow of manure;
spreading it steaming over next year's bare beds.

Finally, she accepted his invitation.
Fruit trees made silhouettes of themselves
and a sickle moon hung from the tip of a beanpole.
Moths approached the opened-up faces of swaying primroses.
He fed her grapes, left them fizzing on her tongue.
They sat silently and very still,
behind glass, but unable to throw stones.

PERMANENT ROSE

Silk. The petals surrounding the gaudy, blowsy, opened-up centre are the deepest, purest, smoothest shades of red. Carmine, alizarin crimson, vermillion, scarlet, cadmium, magenta. Each flower glows like a little lit-up lantern, its silk stretched tight over a wire frame. Pure colours are vivid against the cerulean blue of the sky, bold as windblown triangles strung out in lines of prayer.

Paper. My pencil makes a faint outline on the heavy page, tracing the shape of a rhododendron; faithfully reproducing its construction before the liberation of my paint brush.

Tin. I snap open the little black box of colours and consider the familiar blocks of paint; some worn and shaped into holes and furrows, others barely touched. Prussian blue, burnt umber, yellow ochre, viridian, violet, Payne's grey. And my favourite: permanent rose.

Sable. The tip of a dipped brush moves fluidly, filling in and washing over; loose and transparent or tight and opaque. Colour blooms and blossoms upon damp paper. I try to capture what I see – a rhododendron lighting up its own glossy leaves like a firecracker in the forest; a flower shockingly and wonderfully unafraid.

Poplin. I lay down my painting and stretch out under the *tree of roses*. My skirt and petticoats fall in a circle all around me, pleats and folds pale beneath the heavy flowers. Abandoned, my watercolours fail to match their pristine beauty.

HARVEST

Spikily serrated and knife edge sharp,
exotically alien first time in the flesh.
You hack stickily through crocodile skin,
cut with difficulty into slices and cubes.
Orangey-lemon and boiled sugar sweet,
you refuse to choose the pantry shelf favourite;
pale rings of tinned pineapple grow dusty in rows.

Fruit bowl familiar,
mottle-stained pears fall from August to Autumn.
You watch and wait for the yielding moment
between too sharp crunch and ripeness over blown.
Cool skinned, September's scarce harvest
sees the last of the swallows swooping;
finds yourself and the gardeners praying for a better year.